Contents

Nuclear Power

Electricity is such a big part of our lives we take it for granted. We flip a switch and expect instant power. But did you know that when you use your television or toaster you could well be using electricity from a **nuclear power station**?

One fifth of all the electricity we use is made in nuclear power stations. There are over 400 across the world, most of them in Europe and America. The very first was a small **prototype**, built in 1951.

Uranium contains a lot of energy. Just 1 kg of uranium can make as much heat as 3 million kg of coal. But uranium can be very dangerous.

A thick concrete dome covers the reactor. This stops radiation escaping.

Heat from the reactor makes steam.

Control rods can be pushed in or out of the **reactor**. They control the reactor, slowing it down, or speeding it up.

There are thousands of fuel rods in the **reactor core**.

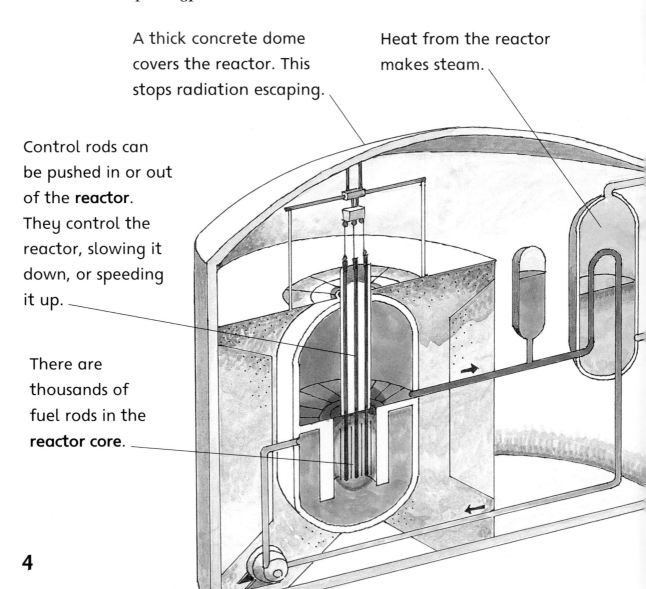

Making electricity

Nuclear power stations work in much the same way as ordinary power stations. They heat water to make steam. The steam turns **turbines** and **generators**. The generators make electricity. But whereas ordinary power stations burn gas, oil or coal to make heat and steam, nuclear power stations use **uranium** fuel rods. These give off energy and heat called **radiation**.

When nuclear power stations work properly they can produce electricity very cheaply. Yet they are very expensive to build. Each new nuclear power station costs around £2 billion. Because of these costs, and the fear of accidents, very few new nuclear power stations are being built today.

Energy from atoms

Atoms are some of the smallest things we know about. You can imagine atoms as tiny building blocks. They group together to make you and everything around you.

Atoms are held together by energy. If an atom is split or knocked, it lets go this energy. In nuclear reactors atoms are split on purpose, so that they will let go of their energy and make heat. Splitting atoms to make energy is called **fission**. Fission is what happens inside a nuclear reactor.

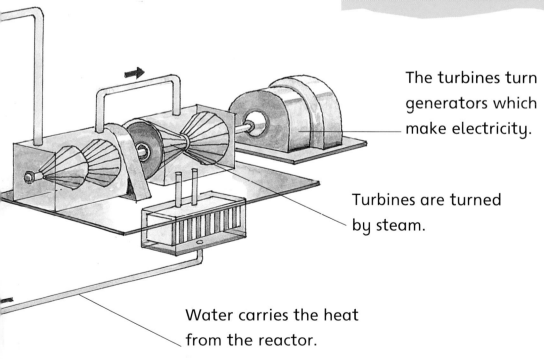

The turbines turn generators which make electricity.

Turbines are turned by steam.

Water carries the heat from the reactor.

When Things Go Wrong

In this book we look at three of the world's worst nuclear accidents, where **nuclear power stations** have burnt and exploded, leaking **radioactive** waste into the land around. We look at what went wrong, and what we can learn to make the world safer.

Built in danger

The **uranium** fuel in today's **reactors** will still be dangerous in 150,000 years' time. If it should escape or leak it will kill or poison every living thing over a huge area. Even small amounts of **radiation** are dangerous, and can increase the risk of **cancer**. High doses of radiation can kill.

Nuclear reactors are designed and built so that accidents shouldn't happen. Strict rules about how they are designed, built and run are set by governments and international authorities such as the Nuclear Energy Agency. But nuclear power stations are still run by people and people make mistakes. They take short cuts, or don't concentrate on what they are doing. They panic. Then there is disaster.

Nuclear accidents

Nuclear reactors cannot explode like nuclear bombs. But if they are not cooled properly they can overheat, and burn. This is the worst sort of nuclear accident and it is called a **meltdown**. In a meltdown the **reactor core** turns into red hot liquid. It can cause explosions in the machinery around it. It can burn through concrete shields. Large amounts of radioactive material can escape.

This is a test nuclear bomb exploding over Bavaria. All this power and destruction comes from splitting atoms. This same power is used in nuclear power stations to make heat.

Other nuclear accidents are less dramatic, but still serious. Radioactive material can escape from the reactor. It can leak through **valves** or broken pipes and get into the steam, water or air that is used to carry heat from the reactor core to the **generators**. From here it can get into the **environment**, and poison food, soil and people.

Nuclear waste

Nuclear waste includes used-up **fuel rods** and leftovers from making nuclear weapons. Such waste stays dangerous for over 10,000 years. One kind of nuclear waste, a metal called **plutonium**, is the most dangerous substance on Earth. One millionth of a gram is enough to cause cancer. No-one has yet decided what to do with the world's nuclear waste. At the moment it is stored – usually at nuclear power stations – while governments work out what to do with it.

On 10 October 1957 one of the two **reactors** at Britain's Windscale **nuclear power station** burst into flames. **Radioactive** dust drifted in clouds from the power station. With the **reactor core** burning red hot, Windscale was on the verge of **meltdown**.

The reactor catches fire

The problems started on 8 October during normal maintenance. The reactor at Windscale was heated up to get rid of a build-up of energy inside it. Operators tried to keep the reactor at 330°C (626°F), the ideal temperature for the job. Yet the controls seemed slow, and the reactor wasn't responding as they expected. By the afternoon of 9 October the temperature inside the reactor had risen to over 400°C (752°F). But the operators did not know this. They could only see the temperature in part of the reactor, not all of it.

It wasn't until 2.30pm on 10 October that the operators realized something, somewhere, was badly wrong. Windscale had begun to burn.

Ron Gausden, who was in charge of the heating-up process, gave orders for his men to push the **fuel rods** from the burning reactor core to stop the fire spreading. But in the heat of the fire the fuel rods had melted and bent, and some seemed stuck fast.

Eight brave men, after having dressed in protective suits and breathing masks, struggled to remove the plugs over each fuel channel.

Using crowbars and even scaffolding poles they pushed the 120 burning fuel rods down their channels and away from the fire. As they moved from one rod to the next, the crowbars they were using came out dripping with **molten** metal.

Nobody showed any signs of fear. You couldn't have seen a better display from the process workers [who moved the burning fuel rods]. They were heroes that night.
Chief Fire Officer, Windscale, 1957

The nuclear reactor at Windscale.

Fire and Luck

At 7pm Tom Tuohy, the deputy manager at Windscale, climbed up onto the **reactor's** roof. Peering through a glass-covered hole called an inspection port he could see the glow of fire. An hour later there were yellow flames. At 11.30pm Tuohy could see blue flames – a sure sign that the fire was getting hotter and it was spreading. Managers at the power station had never dealt with a runaway fire in the reactor before.

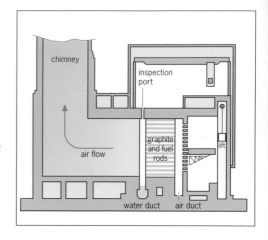

1 On 8 October the train of events leading to disaster begins. Operators try to release heat and energy from **graphite rods** which control the reactor. They don't realize that there is a large risk of the reactor overheating.

2 By 10 October the reactor is overheating, and begins to burn. Eight men struggle to push **fuel rods** along their channels away from the fire. The fire stops spreading, but does not go out.

3 At around 4am carbon dioxide (CO_2) gas is pumped into the reactor. Managers hope that this will smother the fire – but it burns on.

6 On 11 October the wind over Windscale changes. **Radioactive** dust is blown inland. Emergency tests on milk from cows in the area show dangerous levels of radioactive material. But it is four days before proper warnings are given to people living around the power station. All milk is banned from sale over a 5000 hectare area. Farmers pour it away into ditches.

5 At 9am water hoses are turned on. It is only a trickle of water, but it could be enough to cause an explosion. Managers watch tensely. Gradually, as the hoses are turned up, it is clear that Windscale will be safe. The hoses run for 30 hours.

4 By the early hours of 11 October managers at the plant decide to use water on the fire. This is dangerous, and untested – it may cause an explosion. But there is nothing else left to try. They lower hoses into position above the reactor.

Windscale Secrets

After the disaster at Windscale there were investigations and reports by experts. But ordinary people were told almost nothing. It was 26 years before the important facts about what happened, and what more could have happened, were made public.

Government estimates put the number of people who died because of the Windscale disaster at 33. This is the number of extra deaths in the Windscale area thought to have been caused by the disaster. There were also over 200 extra cases of **cancer** caused by Windscale.

But the real facts about how many people suffered because of Windscale will never be known. One reason is that it is hard to tell whether people are ill because of **radiation**, or for some other reason. The effects may take years to show. Children can become ill because their parents were harmed by Windscale – but proving this is very difficult.

In the end what saved Windscale from **meltdown** was the people who worked there, including those who struggled to move the **fuel rods** out of the way of the fire.

> The Report of the Penny Inquiry which was set up to investigate the disaster, said this about the Windscale workers:
>
> *The steps taken to deal with the accident, once it had been discovered, were prompt and efficient and displayed considerable devotion to duty on the part of all concerned.*

Following the Windscale disaster scientists attempted to measure how much radiation had escaped by studying soil samples.

A disaster waiting to happen

Windscale was one of the first **nuclear power stations** ever built. It was designed and built in just four years. The UK government wanted it quickly because it would produce a nuclear waste called **plutonium**. Plutonium is used to make nuclear bombs. The UK wanted to keep up with the USA and the **USSR**, countries which had both built and tested nuclear bombs.

The **reactors** at Windscale were unstable and unpredictable. They used **graphite rods** – like very thick pencil leads – to control the power of the reactor. But over time these **control rods** became swollen and bent. Like batteries they stored heat and energy. Every so often this energy had to be released by heating the reactor. But the danger was that even if this energy was released intentionally by the reactor's operators, the heat could run out of control. On 10 October 1957, this is exactly what happened.

Burn Up!
Disaster at the Three Mile Island Nuclear Power Station, USA

Flashpoint!

It was 4 am. Suddenly the sirens began wailing in the power station control room. A pump feeding the reactor's **cooling system** had failed.

The operators in their white coats kept calm. They had been well trained for emergencies. Pumps had failed before and the reactor had stayed safe, so they remained confident. But a few minutes later red warning lights began to flash. The whole cooling system in the reactor had failed.

In the early hours of 28 March 1979 a **reactor** at Three Mile Island **nuclear power station** in Pennsylvania, USA, began to overheat. It seemed that **meltdown** was only minutes away. There was panic across the area. No-one died, but it is still not really known whether there has been a significant effect on people living in the area.

In just 15 seconds the temperature in the reactor had rocketed by 300°C (572°F). Emergency pumps should have started, pumping cooling water around the reactor. Nothing happened. Now the operators weren't so calm. In the confusion a further emergency pump was accidentally shut down. The temperature in the reactor reached 2700°C (4892°F). The reactor's protective walls began to fall apart. **Radioactive** steam spewed from a waste tank outside the reactor into the **environment**. All this happened in eight minutes.

Mystery bubble

The fire in the reactor caused a mystery bubble to collect in the reactor building. It contained hydrogen, an explosive gas. Experts feared it could **ignite** and blow the roof off the reactor. But as they tried to decide why it was there, and how to deal with it, it began to shrink on its own. Luck had prevented an even greater disaster.

Thousands of people fled from Three Mile Island when news of the disaster came out. They were afraid of the **radiation** that might escape from the power station.

15

Emergency

It took just eight minutes for the **reactor** at Three Mile Island to reach **meltdown** temperature of 3600°C (6512°F). A whole series of instruments, computers and **valves** failed to work. People made mistakes, and very quickly lost control. 'It seemed to go on and on, surprise after surprise', said **radiation** protection supervisor Thomas Mulleavy afterwards.

There were two protective concrete shells covering the reactor. These were meant to hold in any explosions or leaks of **radioactive** material. The reactor burnt through one shell, spilling large amounts of radioactive fuel and gases into the outer shell. Some of these escaped into the **environment**. If the reactor had burnt through the outer shell there would have been a massive loss of life.

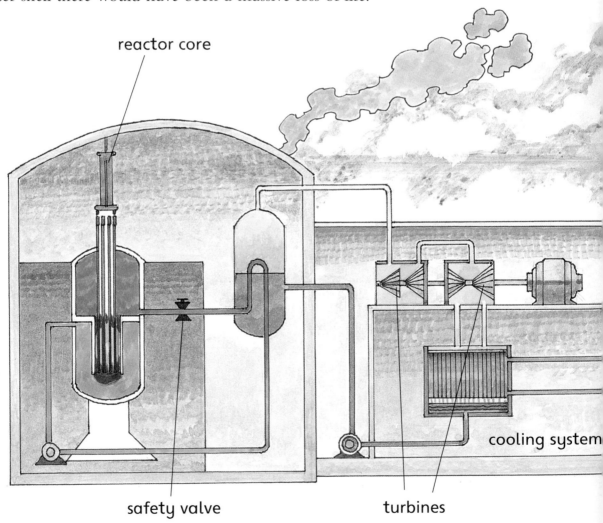

reactor core

safety valve

turbines

cooling system

1 At 4am on 28 March 1979 a water pump fails. The reactor begins to overheat. The emergency **cooling system** also fails. In minutes the reactor begins 'meltdown'.

2 Operators realize that vital valves aren't working. They trigger these by hand. Water floods through into the reactor. The reactor is saved from meltdown, but it is too late to stop a radioactive cloud drifting towards the nearby town of Harrisburg.

3 Water used to cool the reactor leaks into the reactor building. It is highly radioactive. A 400,000 gallon (almost 2 million litres) waste tank of less radioactive water has to be dumped into the Susquehanna River to make room for it.

4 The emergency is made public at 11am on 28 March. Panic breaks out as people flee the invisible poison. The telephone system is jammed. Troops move in and 140,000 people flee the area. The American President declares a **national emergency**. Pregnant women and children living within 13km of the power station are most at risk from the radioactivity, so they are told to leave.

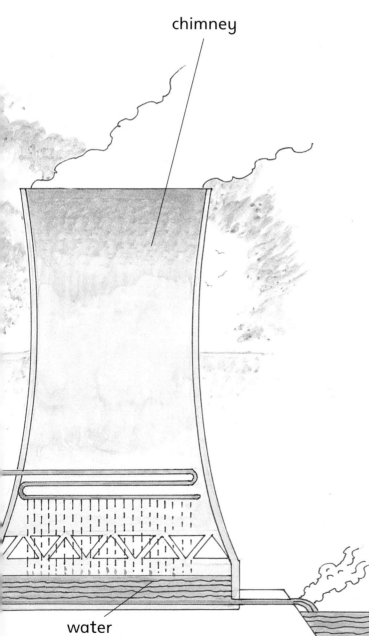

chimney

water

Susquehanna River

What Went Wrong?

It was two weeks before the Three Mile Island **nuclear power station** was declared safe. Then the enquiries began. Why had it happened? Had the disaster been an accident, or was someone or something to blame?

The $1 billion mistake

The disaster at Three Mile Island changed everything for nuclear power. People in America had found out it wasn't as cheap, clean or safe as experts had said it was. Many no longer trusted this new technology.

New safety rules were brought in including fire equipment, new emergency plans, extra training for operators, and new inspectors for each nuclear power station. Many nuclear power stations had to close because they couldn't afford to meet the cost of the new rules. Orders for new nuclear power stations being built in America were cancelled.

There had been a record of near accidents at the Three Mile Island plant. Twice before important **valves** in the **cooling system** had failed to work. These were the same valves that were involved in the disaster. It became clear that although the power company which ran Three Mile Island power station had known there was a risk, they had failed to act.

Experts also found that the instruments the operators relied on to tell them what was happening in the **reactor** were very slow. Sometimes they gave readings that were one and a half hours out of date, which meant that the reactor's operators would not know how bad an emergency was until it was too late.

Three Mile Island also had another problem. The nuclear power station cost a huge amount of money to build. In order to recoup some of this money, Three Mile Island was run almost constantly. Even safety checks were carried out as the plant ran. Repairs were often left to official shutdowns, so that no money-making electricity would be lost. Safety at Three Mile Island was ignored too often. In the end it caused disaster.

In the film *The China Syndrome* two TV news-reporters (played by Jack Lemmon and Jane Fonda) chase a story about a scare at a nuclear power station caused by lies and poor safety regulations.

The China Syndrome

Not long before the disaster at Three Mile Island a film had begun showing in American cinemas. *The China Syndrome* was about a nuclear accident – a **'meltdown'**. When they saw the film, experts from the American nuclear industry said the accident in the film couldn't happen. At Three Mile Island it did.

Meltdown!
The Chernobyl Nuclear Power Station Disaster
USSR

On 26 April 1986 a **reactor** at the Chernobyl **nuclear power station** exploded. A deadly **radioactive** cloud spewed from the burning reactor and hundreds of people were killed. Two hundred thousand people were affected. Even today people are still dying from **radiation** unleashed during the disaster.

Steps to disaster

On 25 April 1986 scientists at the Chernobyl nuclear plant, Ukraine, in the **USSR** began a safety test on reactor number 4. During the test, the reactor's emergency **cooling system** was switched off.

Sitting in the control room, the operator began the test. First he slowed the reactor down, and reduced power. The emergency cooling system was disconnected. But then, at 2pm, electricity workers at Kiev requested that the test in the reactor be delayed because they needed electricity. The Chernobyl staff brought the reactor back up to normal power. But the emergency cooling system was not turned back on.

This was the first of a string of serious errors. At 1.23am the next morning the situation became critical. Reactor power surged. Extreme heat began to break up the reactor from the inside. It was reaching **meltdown**, and there was nothing anyone could do to stop it. Machinery, pipes and tanks around the reactor exploded.

Showers of burning concrete and deadly lumps of reactor tore through the roof. Thirty fires began to burn across the power station, and clouds of deadly **radioactive** gas and smoke drifted up into the sky.

20

Explosion at Chernobyl. The wreckage is what remains of the reactor. Standing near it, even for a few minutes, meant absorbing enough radiation to kill you.

We heard heavy explosions! You can't imagine what's happening here with all the deaths and fire. I'm here 32km from it, and in fact I don't know what to do. I don't know if our leaders know what to do, because this is a real disaster. Please tell the world to help us.
(Transmission reported by Annis Kofman, Dutch radio enthusiast, 29 April.)

Heroes of the fire

Many of the fire-fighters, soldiers, pilots and doctors on duty at Chernobyl knew the dangers of radiation. They knew that without protective suits or breathing masks they would become ill or die. There was no protective clothing available, but they carried on anyway. In under an hour many were already too ill to carry on.

Nuclear Inferno

Politicians and officials had confidently said that disaster would never happen at the Chernobyl **nuclear power station**. When it did, no-one was ready. Fire crews and soldiers had no protective suits, or breathing masks to protect them from **radiation**. For 10 days they battled with the immense heat of the burning **reactor**, shovelling sand into bags for helicopter pilots to drop over it.

1   The disaster at Chernobyl begins on 25 April 1986 with a safety test on the reactor. Operators make serious mistakes. Cooling pumps are operating beyond their capability. At 1.19am on 26 April the test should have been stopped. But operators override the automatic shutdown and carry on. There are only seven or eight **control rods** left in the reactor. The safe minimum is 30.

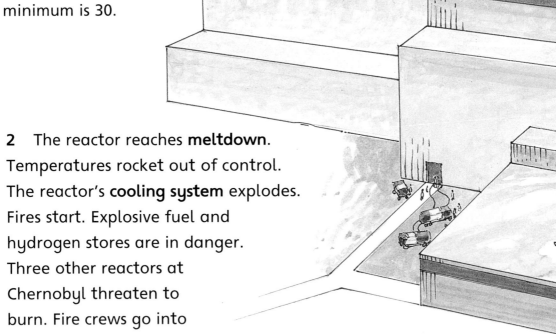

2   The reactor reaches **meltdown**. Temperatures rocket out of control. The reactor's **cooling system** explodes. Fires start. Explosive fuel and hydrogen stores are in danger. Three other reactors at Chernobyl threaten to burn. Fire crews go into action at 1.30am.

5 A poisonous cloud of radiation floats over the Ukraine and on into Europe. The wind and rain deposit radiation over Welsh hills. In Greece there is panic from people afraid of radiation poisoning. In Germany milk sales are banned because cows are eating radioactive grass. In Italy tonnes of fresh vegetables are dumped because of fears that they are **contaminated** with radioactivity from Chernobyl.

4 Chernobyl and Pripyat, the nearest towns to the disaster, are **evacuated**. In Pripyat 40,000 people leave their homes in under three hours. They take only what they can carry. They can never go home again.

3 By 5 am the fires are out – only the reactor itself is still burning. Helicopters work in shifts, dropping sand from 50 m above the reactor building. They are trying to smother fire in the reactor, and to stop **radioactive** material escaping into the **environment**.

Deadly Secret

The fire in the Chernobyl **reactor** burnt for 10 days. It spewed 50 tonnes of deadly **radioactive** material into the air. Yet for two days the outside world knew nothing. The government of the **USSR** tried to keep the worst disaster in nuclear history a secret. They wanted no criticism of their **nuclear power stations,** or of their safety policies.

The first warning to the outside world came on 28 April when workers at a Swedish nuclear power station measured frightening levels of **radiation**. It soon became clear that the radiation was coming from the USSR. At 9pm a four-line news item about Chernobyl was carried on USSR TV. The 'accident' was official. But the secrecy had exposed hundreds of thousands of people to increased risks.

Who was to blame?

Six workers at the Chernobyl power station were put on trial for the disaster. The six workers were sentenced to a total of 40 years in prison for their careless neglect of safety – they often played games or wrote letters while on duty. The USSR court put most of the blame on the managing director of the power station, Viktor Bryukhanov. Bryukhanov said at his trial, 'With so many deaths I can't say I'm completely innocent.'

Thousands of people waited for buses to leave Chernobyl.

Workers built this giant concrete coffin over the destroyed reactor at Chernobyl nuclear power station.

Impossible clean-up

At Chernobyl the first job was to stop more radioactive material from escaping. When the fires were out, soldiers and miners built a huge concrete coffin to enclose the reactor. Miners tunnelled under the reactor, building a giant saucer to stop the reactor melting through the floor of the building and into the ground, where it could **contaminate** the water of the whole region. Then over 600,000 people set about cleaning up the area. But no complete clean-up was really possible.

Dead land

A circle of land 64 km around Chernobyl power station is still radioactive. It will remain closed to the outside world for 150 years. Only those who still work at the Chernobyl power station – where amazingly other reactors are still running – visit the area. Today governments in Europe still believe Chernobyl is unsafe and they want it closed.

Lessons from Disaster

Ever since the first **nuclear power station** was built in the 1950s people have feared accidents. Most accidents have not been serious, but some may have been kept secret. Governments and power companies do not like to admit that they have come close to disaster. They fear the reaction of the public.

The dangers of secrecy

Secrecy is one of nuclear power's big problems. At Chernobyl in 1986 authorities kept the accident secret, even though for several days this put thousands of people at risk. At Windscale in 1957 it took four days before local people were warned not to drink milk **contaminated** by **radiation**. This history of secrecy means that many people do not trust nuclear power stations, or the people that run them. After the accident at Three Mile Island, people who had been **evacuated** from the site were suspicious of government claims that it was safe to go home. They simply didn't believe that any government would tell the truth about nuclear accidents.

Nuclear power stations like Sellafield, England (above) do not pollute the air with smoke – but they can still be dangerous if the correct safety measures are not observed.

Is it safe?

Supporters of nuclear power say that new **reactor** designs are safer. Accidents are becoming less likely. Nuclear power, when it works properly, is less damaging to the **environment** than burning coal or oil to make electricity. And what else will we burn to make electricity when coal, oil and gas run out?

Anti-nuclear campaigners stress the dangers of nuclear power and the fact that there are safer and cleaner ways of making electricity. There is also the problem of nuclear waste, which remains **radioactive** for thousands of years.

Future risks

Many of the old reactors that are still working are known to be dangerous. Such reactors are mostly in the countries that made up the **USSR**. Some governments in Europe, and in America, are paying to have them closed down. But others still operate. In 1986 James Asseltine, then head of the US Nuclear Regulatory Authority, said: 'I have to advise **Congress** that there is a 45 per cent chance of another serious nuclear accident within the next 20 years.'

Many environmental organizations, such as **Greenpeace**, are opposed to nuclear power because of nuclear waste and the risk of accidents. This 'die-in' protest took place at Doodewaard nuclear power plant, the Netherlands, in 1994.

The World's Worst Nuclear Disaster

Chalk River, Canada, 12 December 1952 Partial **meltdown** in **reactor core**. No leaks, but the first known nuclear accident.

Kyshtym, Russia, 1957 (exact date kept secret) Nuclear waste container explodes. Thirty villages disappear from **USSR** maps. It is estimated that more than 8000 people die as a result over the next 32 years.

Windscale, (now called Sellafield) UK, 7 October 1957 Fire in the reactor core. **Radiation** leak. Estimated 33 deaths over the following years.

Idaho Falls, USA, 3 January 1961 Steam explosion in an experimental military **reactor**. Three soldiers killed.

Browns Ferry, USA, 22 March 1975 Fire in reactor wiring. No leak.

Three Mile Island, USA, 28 March 1979 Partial meltdown in reactor core. Radiation leak. No deaths, but the danger to local people is still unknown.

Tsuruga, Japan, 8 March 1981 Radioactive water leaks from reactor. Workers receive high doses of radiation.

Gore, USA, 4 January 1986 Worker killed by bursting container of nuclear material. Radiation leak. 100 people admitted to hospital. No known deaths.

Chernobyl, USSR, 26 April 1986 Meltdown of reactor core. More than 200 people killed, perhaps 200,000 people at risk from radiation.

This map shows the countries which have **nuclear power stations**, and how many they have.

Radiation sickness

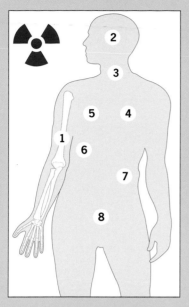

1 bone marrow damage
  – people lose the
  ability to fight disease
2 unborn children suffer
  brain damage
3 thyroid cancer
4 lung cancer
5 breast cancer
6 liver failure
7 kidney failure
8 future children may
  suffer diseases

People exposed to a lot of radiation become sick. Many die within days or months. Others develop **cancer** and other diseases later in life.

On the nuclear map

There are over 400 nuclear reactors in the world. The USA, France, Japan and the UK have the largest number of reactors.

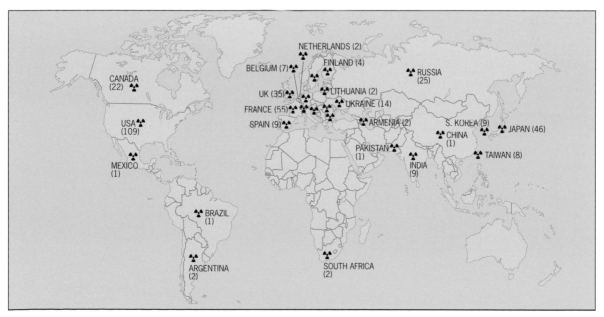

CANADA (22)

NETHERLANDS (2)
BELGIUM (7)
FINLAND (4)
RUSSIA (25)
UK (35)
LITHUANIA (2)
FRANCE (55)
UKRAINE (14)
SPAIN (9)
ARMENIA (2)
S. KOREA (9)
JAPAN (46)
USA (109)
CHINA (1)
PAKISTAN (1)
TAIWAN (8)
MEXICO (1)
INDIA (9)
BRAZIL (1)
ARGENTINA (2)
SOUTH AFRICA (2)

Glossary

cancer disease in which a group of cells grows and multiplies rapidly, killing nearby tissue. It often kills.

Congress national law-making body of the USA

contaminated something which has a dangerous substance on or in it

control rods rods pushed in and out of a reactor to speed it up, or slow it down

cooling system pipe and tanks that circulate water around a reactor or other machine to keep it cool

environment external surroundings; the land, water and air around us

evacuate move people away from a dangerous place until it is safe for them to return

fission splitting atoms, by firing other atoms into them

fuel rods rods of a metal such as uranium which are used as fuel inside a reactor. Fuel rods are put together in bundles and loaded into a reactor.

generator machine which makes electricity when it is turned. Bicycle dynamos are small generators.

graphite rods rods, a bit like very thick pencil leads, which control the power of the reactor (see control rods)

Greenpeace is an international organization which campaigns on a range of environmental issues. Its members often use dramatic tactics to bring attention to their causes.

ignite set on fire

meltdown when a reactor burns and turns into a red hot liquid

molten melted, turned to hot sticky liquid

national emergency indicates a serious emergency when emergency services nationwide should be on standby, ready to help if necessary

nuclear power station an electricity generating station which uses nuclear energy

plutonium metal element produced inside nuclear reactors. It is both poisonous and radioactive and is used in nuclear bombs, and inside reactors.

prototype working model of a new invention

radiation energy moving in the form of electromagnetic waves

radiation sickness symptoms and illnesses people get when they receive big doses of radiation; these include vomiting and burns

radioactive/radioactivity something which gives off particles and rays of radiation

reactor large tank or building holding the pipes and machinery needed to make nuclear energy

reactor core centre of a reactor holding the fuel rods and control rods

turbine machine or wheel driven by a stream of gas, water or steam

uranium grey metal element, heavier than lead and used as fuel in nuclear reactors

USSR Union of Soviet Socialist Republics. This country no longer exists but split up in 1991. Former republics joined together as the Commonwealth of Independent States (CIS) in the same year.

valve small flap or door inside a pipe that turns on or off like a tap

Index